ARMOR *for the* MIND

Finding Strength, Peace, and Freedom in Christ

JOY DAVILA

Armor
for the
Mind

Armor for the Mind
by Joy Davila

instagram.com/joywalkingbyfaith

For quantity discounts, please contact: joy.davila7@gmail.com

ISBN:
Paperback: 979-8-9952348-0-7
Hardcover: 979-8-9952348-1-4
Ebook: 979-8-9952348-2-1

Photography: Daniela Murray · YourMomentsByDaniela.com
Design: Bookable Media · BookableMedia.com

Dedication

To my parents, who constantly saved me and loved me without fail.
And to my husband, who met me as I came out of the darkness
and walked with me into the light.

CONTENTS

INTRODUCTION

I never thought I would be here, writing a book about freedom and transformation. There was a time when my life felt like it was spiraling in the opposite direction, weighed down by addiction, shame, and the never-ending voice of negativity in my mind. My thoughts told me I would never change, that I wasn't strong enough, and that my past would always define me. Maybe you've heard that same voice before, whispering lies into your heart.

But here's the truth: I am living proof that change is possible. Over ten years ago, I walked into a church and tired of fighting battles I could never win on my own. I laid my burdens at the feet of Jesus, and that decision changed everything. It wasn't overnight, and it wasn't easy, but with God's help, I learned how to renew my mind and shift from destructive, negative thoughts to thoughts rooted in His truth.

This book is not just about me. It's about you. If you've ever felt stuck in the same cycle of fear, doubt, or addiction, I want you to know there is a way out. The journey begins in your mind. The Bible tells us that transformation starts with the renewing of our thoughts, and I believe with all my heart that if God could do it for me, He can do it for you.

We are living in uncertain and difficult times. The tragic loss of Charlie Kirk reminds us that now more than ever we must lean into our faith and put on the full armor of God each day. The world is dark, and the enemy is relentless, but God has given us everything we need to stand firm against the lies and attacks that come our way. Renewing our minds is not just a personal choice, it is a spiritual weapon. When we guard our thoughts and anchor them in God's Word, we are equipping ourselves to face whatever comes.

In these pages, I will share my story and the steps I took to replace toxic thoughts with life-giving ones. You'll find practical exercises, faith-building encouragement, and scriptures that will help you fight back against lies and claim the victory that is already yours in Christ.

This is not just a book about positive thinking. This is a book about God's power to transform a life from the inside out. My prayer is that as you read, you don't just learn new ideas, but that you feel the presence of the Holy Spirit guiding you toward freedom.

Get ready. You are about to step into a new way of living. One filled with peace, joy, and the kind of victory that only comes from God.

Verse

"Finally, be strong in the Lord and in his mighty power. Put on the full armor of God, so that you can take your stand against the devil's schemes."

— Ephesians 6:10–11 (NIV)

Chapter One

The Battle of the Mind

Every day, thousands of thoughts rush through. Some hopeful and uplifting, others heavy and destructive. The truth is that your life moves in the direction of your strongest thoughts. If those thoughts are negative, you'll find yourself stuck in fear, shame, or self-doubt. But if those thoughts are aligned with God's truth, you'll discover peace, joy, and the strength to walk in victory.

For almost a decade of my life, my thoughts pushed me down the wrong path. Lies filled my mind, telling me to party harder, numb the emptiness, and ignore the ache in my soul. I surrounded myself with toxic friends and believed them over the loving voices of my parents and sister. I thought I was just having fun, but really, I was sinking deeper into a dangerous life I didn't even realize was destroying me.

For years, I followed those lies in my mind. I wasn't even aware of how far I was drifting until I almost lost my life with the wrong combination of choices. It was in that moment of brokenness that I fell to the feet of Jesus, and He lifted me up. I never looked back. But here's what I've learned through all of that pain: thoughts are not permanent. They can be challenged and they can be replaced. And when I finally surrendered them to God, He showed me I was never alone. He had been carrying me through those dangerous waters the entire time.

When I look back now, I realize the battle wasn't happening around me, it was happening inside me. The mind is a battlefield where faith and fear wrestle for control. Every lie I believed gave the enemy power, and every truth I declared gave that power back to God. It's why what you think matters so much. Your mind can become a prison, or it can become a place of peace, but only when surrendered to Him.

Recognizing the Power of a Thought

"Your thoughts can build your world or break it."

A single thought can lead to a chain reaction. Consider this: Thought: "I'll never get better."→ Emotion: Hopelessness. → Action: Giving up, returning to old habits. Now imagine the opposite: Thought: "With God, all things are possible." → Emotion: Hope. → Action: Taking one more step forward, refusing to quit.

I began to see how my life reflected the stories I told myself. If I said I couldn't change, I stayed stuck. If I believed God could heal me, even in my weakest moments, I found the courage to get back up. Our minds are powerful because they agree with something, either truth or lies. And whichever one we feed, it grows stronger.

So what are you feeding your thoughts with? Are you filling your mind with worry, comparison, and what-ifs, or are you filling it with scripture, prayer, and gratitude? Every thought has a destination. Choose yours wisely.

Exposing the Enemy's Strategy

"The mind is the devil's favorite playground, but it doesn't have to be."

The enemy doesn't need to destroy your body to defeat you… all he needs is access to your mind. He plants seeds of fear, doubt, and condemnation. If left unchecked, those seeds grow into strongholds that keep you bound. But God gives us weapons to fight back. His Word tells us to take captive every thought to make it obedient to Christ (2 Corinthians 10:5). When a thought enters your mind, you don't have to accept it. Measure it against God's truth and decide whether it stays or goes.

The more I learned to recognize those lies, the quicker I could reject them. I started noticing thoughts like, "You'll never be free," or "You're not good enough," and I would immediately answer them with truth. I had to train my spirit to respond instead of reacting. Every time I opened the Word, it became like armor protecting my peace.

Taking Every Thought Captive

"Victory starts when you confront your thoughts, not when you run from them."

Here's a simple process I started using when negative thoughts come:

1. Catch It: Notice when a negative or destructive thought enters.
2. Challenge It: Ask, "Is this what God says about me?"
3. Change It: Replace it with scripture or a positive truth.

Example: Thought: "I am worthless." Truth: "I praise you because I am fearfully and wonderfully made." (Psalm 139:14, NIV)

This process transformed my thinking. It wasn't overnight, it was daily discipline. Some mornings I woke up still feeling unworthy, but I learned that feelings don't define truth. Faith does. Over time, my old patterns began to lose power, and I started walking in freedom.

Reflection

What negative thought has been repeated in your mind lately? Write it down. Then, next to it, write the truth of God's Word that cancels it out.

Prayer

Lord, help me recognize the battle in my mind. Teach me to take every thought captive and make it obedient to You. Fill my mind with Your truth and silence the lies of the enemy. Amen.

Verse

> *"For though we live in the world, we do not wage war as the world does. The weapons we fight with are not the weapons of the world. On the contrary, they have divine power to demolish strongholds."*
>
> — 2 Corinthians 10:3–4 (NIV)

[illegible]

[illegible] Caption

[illegible]

Reflection

[illegible]

Prayer

[illegible]

Chapter Two

Identifying Lies

Once we learn to recognize that the battle begins in our mind, the next step is uncovering the lies that have taken root there. Every stronghold, every doubt, every fear often starts as a single deceptive thought. And while the battle may begin in our mind, freedom begins when truth takes its place. The enemy knows that if he can control your thoughts, he can control your direction. That's why his greatest weapon isn't always destruction, it's deception.

When people picture the devil at work, they often imagine something dramatic like an obvious attack, a storm, or a tragedy. But the enemy is far more subtle than we give him credit for. His most dangerous weapon isn't always destruction, it's deception. The lies we believe about ourselves, about God, and about our future are what keep us trapped. They are like invisible chains, holding us back even when freedom is right in front of us.

For years, I didn't realize how much of my life was shaped by lies. Lies like: "You'll never change." "You've messed up too much for God to forgive you." "You're not good enough." These weren't dramatic attacks by the accuser; they were whispers in my mind. Lies that seemed small but grew stronger the more I agreed with them. The enemy rarely shouts; he whispers until you mistake his lies for your own thoughts.

Recognizing the Whisper

One of the most important steps in renewing your mind is learning to recognize where your thoughts come from. Not every thought is true. Not every idea deserves your agreement. Some are planted by the enemy to steer you off course. The Bible tells us that the devil is "a liar and the father of lies" (John 8:44, NIV). If he can convince you to accept his lies, he doesn't need to destroy you because you'll do it yourself by living in agreement with deception.

I remember seasons where I was doing well, working hard, praying more, and feeling like I was finally walking in the right direction and suddenly, a quiet voice would whisper, "Who do you think you are?" or "You'll never really change." Those thoughts didn't come from me, but for years I treated them as my own voice. That's how the enemy works: he doesn't need to shout; he just needs you to agree. Once he gets your agreement, the lie begins to take root.

Learning to recognize those whispers is one of the greatest spiritual disciplines you can develop. When that voice tells you that you are not enough, measure it against what God has said. When it tells you that your past defines your worth, remind yourself that you are made new in Christ. Truth always exposes deception, and light always drives out darkness.

Lies About Identity

The enemy loves to attack our identity. If he can get you to believe you are worthless, unloved, or too broken, then you'll never step into the purpose God has for you. But God says something different: You are chosen. You are loved. You are redeemed. The contrast between what the enemy says and what God says is the difference between bondage and freedom.

I used to believe my worth was tied to my performance, how much I achieved, how well I looked, or whether people approved of me. When I failed, I believed I was a failure. When I disappointed someone, I thought I was unlovable. But God began to teach me that identity isn't built on perfection; it's built on position and being His child. When you understand who you are in Him, the lies lose their grip.

That shift doesn't happen overnight. It happens little by little, every time you choose to believe truth over lies. When you remind yourself that you are created in the image of God, fearfully and wonderfully made, something changes inside of you. Confidence begins to rise. Peace begins to settle. The enemy can't manipulate someone who knows their worth in Christ.

Lies About God

Another common tactic is to distort how we see God. The enemy whispers, "God doesn't care about you. He's distant. He's disappointed in you." But Scripture shows us the opposite. God is near to the brokenhearted (Psalm 34:18, NIV). He is a loving Father who runs to His children when they return to Him (Luke 15:20, NIV). If the enemy can twist how, you see God, he can keep you from running to the very One who can heal you.

I once believed that God tolerated me but didn't delight in me. I thought He loved me in theory, but not in practice. That lie kept me distant, praying from a place of guilt instead of relationship. But the truth is, God's love isn't based on performance, it's based on His nature. He doesn't just love; He is love. When I started seeing Him as a Father who wanted to spend time with me, my faith deepened. It stopped being about trying to earn His approval and became about walking in His presence.

Lies About Your Future

The enemy wants you to believe your past defines your future. He says, "You'll never be free. You'll always be the same." But God says, "I am doing a new thing! Now it springs up; do you not perceive it?" (Isaiah 43:19, NIV). When you believe God's promises about your future, the grip of the past begins to lose its power.

I used to live in fear that my mistakes would always follow me, that my story was too tainted to be redeemed. But God has a way of using the very things that once broke you to build something beautiful. Every scar becomes a story of His faithfulness. Every detour becomes a testimony of His grace. You may not see the full picture right now, but trust that the Author of your life is still writing.

When you begin to identify the lies about your future and replace them with the truth of God's Word, hope rises again. Instead of saying, "I can't," you start to declare, "Through Christ, I can." Instead of fearing what's ahead, you start to anticipate what God will do next. That's how faith begins to transform your outlook, it trades anxiety for expectancy.

Reflection

What lies have you been believing about yourself, about God, or about your future? Write them down. Then, next to each lie, write a scripture that reveals the truth.

Prayer

Lord, open my eyes to the lies I have been believing. Help me to see clearly where the enemy has deceived me, and replace those lies with Your truth. Remind me daily of who I am in You, and give me the strength to reject every false word spoken over my life. Amen.

Verse

> *"You belong to your father, the devil, and you want to carry out your father's desires. He was a murderer from the beginning, not holding to the truth, for there is no truth in him. When he lies, he speaks his native language, for he is a liar and the father of lies."*
>
> — John 8:44 (NIV)

Chapter Three

The Subtle Creep of the Enemy

The enemy rarely storms into our lives with obvious destruction. More often, he slips in quietly, unnoticed, little by little. A thought here. A compromise there. A small habit that doesn't seem dangerous at first glance. And before long, we're entangled in patterns that weigh us down and pull us away from God's truth. The enemy doesn't need to wreck your life all at once. He only needs you to stop paying attention. His strategy is slow erosion, not sudden explosion.

For me, it wasn't just the parties or the reckless choices, it was the way I let my guard down day after day. Each decision seemed harmless at the time, but together they built a life I didn't recognize anymore. I didn't realize that the thoughts I was feeding were shaping the life I was living. The enemy never shouted; he whispered. And slowly, those whispers became my reality. What began as excitement and freedom eventually became chains I couldn't see but could feel.

There's a moment I'll never forget. I was riding home with a man I wasn't in love with, on the back of his Ninja motorcycle after a night of drinking at a festival forty-five minutes away. The air was cold, the road dark, and the engine roared beneath us. He sped down the highway like nothing could touch him, weaving through cars at terrifying speed while I clung to him, realizing that if I let go, I'd be gone. And then the thought hit me... if I died in that moment, would he even care? My heart raced, not just from fear, but from the emptiness that came with it. I whispered a prayer through the noise, asking God to keep me safe. And He did. It was moments like that when I began to see clearly. God had been protecting me long before I was walking with Him.

That night changed me. I didn't have an instant transformation or a blinding light moment, but it planted something deep inside. It planted a conviction. I realized I had been chasing a high that was killing me from the inside out. Addiction isn't freeing; it's binding. It promises escape but delivers emptiness. I used to chase a high, but now I chase Jesus. Every time I look back on that ride, I see it as a picture of my life at the time: holding onto something dangerous, afraid to let go, and praying that God would somehow save me. And He did. His mercy caught me before my choices destroyed me.

Every sin, every compromise, begins with a whisper. The enemy never forces himself into your life, he invites you to open the door. He starts small because small feels safe. A little comparison. A little bitterness. A small habit you promise to control tomorrow. And slowly, he builds his foundation until the lie feels like truth. By the time you realize you've drifted, you're already far from the shore. That's how he works! Not through chaos, but through comfort.

Everyday Disguises

The devil doesn't always show up in dramatic temptations. Sometimes he works through ordinary things: how we talk to ourselves, how we handle food and our bodies, or the way we let comparison steal our joy. If left unchecked, these small battles become open doors for the enemy to take ground in our lives. He hides behind what feels normal, knowing we're less likely to fight what we don't see as dangerous.

Maybe it's scrolling social media and feeling that slow ache of comparison. Maybe it's staying too busy to spend time in prayer. Maybe it's convincing that one more drink, one more late night, one more compromise won't matter. That's the subtle creep. The shift from conviction to complacency. Before long, what once felt wrong starts to feel normal. And when sin starts to feel normal, that's when we're in danger.

Recognizing Subtle Attacks

One of the most important lessons I learned is that not every thought or desire comes from me. Some are planted to pull me off course. Ephesians 6 reminds us that our battle is not against flesh and blood, but against spiritual forces. That means what looks like a simple craving, a careless word, or a moment of self-criticism can sometimes be part of a much bigger spiritual battle. The enemy knows your weak spots. He studies your patterns. He uses the same temptations until you believe they're just part of who you are.

But here's the truth… the accuser can only be defeated by the Advocate. Satan may accuse, but Jesus defends. When we rely on our own strength, we lose the battle. But when we stand behind the shield of faith and use the Word of God as our weapon, the enemy must flee. Christ isn't just our refuge; He is our weapon. He doesn't just protect us from the storm, He teaches us how to stand through it.

Guarding Against the Drift

Drift happens slowly. Nobody wakes up one morning and decides to walk away from God. It begins with small distractions, small lies, and small excuses. That's why God calls us to put on the full armor daily, so we can stand firm even in the small things. Staying alert doesn't mean living in fear, it means living in awareness. It means pausing long enough to ask, "Is this thought from God, or is it pulling me away from Him?" When we ask that question, we give the Holy Spirit room to guide us back before we drift too far.

The good news is that even when we drift, God doesn't lose sight of us. His love is relentless. He doesn't shame us into obedience; He draws us back through grace. He shows us the difference between conviction and condemnation. Conviction invites us home; condemnation tells us we're too far gone. But there's no such thing as too far gone when it comes to God's mercy.

Reflection

Where have small compromises or subtle lies been creeping into your life? Write them down. Then ask God to reveal which ones are pulling you away from Him, even if they seem harmless on the surface.

Prayer

Lord, help me to see the subtle ways the enemy tries to creep into my life. Give me discernment to recognize his lies and strength to resist them. Teach me to put on Your armor every day so I may stand firm in Your truth. Amen.

Verse

"Be alert and of sober mind. Your enemy the devil prowls around like a roaring lion looking for someone to devour."

— 1 Peter 5:8 (NIV)

Chapter Four

Prayer that Transforms

Prayer is not just a religious habit; it's the lifeline that connects us to the power of God. For years, I didn't pray because I didn't think God was listening. I thought He was too far away or too disappointed in me to care. But the truth is, He was always near, waiting for me to talk to Him.

I remember some of my first prayers in recovery. They weren't fancy. I didn't know the "right" words. Sometimes all I could manage was, "God, help me." And that was enough. Because prayer isn't about impressing God with long speeches; it's about opening your heart to Him.

Honest Conversations with God

God doesn't want the cleaned-up version of you. He wants the real you, the raw, hurting, unpolished version. When I finally prayed with honesty instead of performing, I felt Him begin to heal my heart.

It's easy to think prayer must sound holy or poetic, but God values authenticity more than anything else. Some of my most powerful prayers came through tears, broken sentences, or even silence. When you invite Him into your struggles, He meets you there.

I used to think I had to hide the messy parts of my story when I prayed. I thought I needed to earn His approval before I could approach Him. But prayer taught me that I could come boldly, even in my brokenness. The Bible says we can "approach God's throne of grace with confidence" (Hebrews 4:16), and that truth changed everything for me.

Over time, prayer became more than a rituality, it became a relationship. I started to see God not as a distant judge but as a loving Father who wanted to hear my voice. When I sat quietly in His presence, pouring out the pain I'd tried to bury for years, something supernatural happened. His peace began to replace my anxiety. His love started to dissolve my shame.

Sometimes I still struggle to find the words, but I've learned that prayer isn't about perfection, it's about presence. It's the art of being still long enough for your soul to remember who it belongs to.

Listening to His Voice

Prayer isn't just talking; it's listening. In the stillness, God began to remind me who I was in Him… chosen, loved, redeemed. Sometimes He spoke through scripture, other times through a whisper in my spirit, and often through people He placed around me.

Listening to God requires a quiet heart. The world is loud and full of distractions. Our phones buzz, our thoughts race, and our worries compete for attention. But when I learned to quiet the noise, I discovered that God was speaking all along, I just wasn't tuned in.

There were days I'd sit in silence with worship music playing softly in the background, asking God to show me one thing: "What do You want me to know right now?" And He always did. Maybe not in the way I expected, but always in the way I needed.

Sometimes His answer was peace. Sometimes it was conviction. And sometimes, it was patience or an invitation to trust His timing when I wanted to rush ahead. Prayer doesn't always give you immediate answers, but it always gives you perspective. It realigns your thoughts with His truth.

Over time, I noticed how prayers began to change the way I saw everything. It gave me discernment to see people through compassion instead of criticism, to view obstacles as opportunities, and to recognize that delays were often divine protection.

Breaking Cycles with Prayer

Every time I faced the temptation to return to old habits, prayer became my weapon. Instead of running back to what was familiar, I ran to God. And slowly, the cycle began to break.

Prayer gives you power over the patterns that once controlled you. It shifts your focus from what you *can't* change to the One who *can.* The moment you pray, heaven gets involved in your story. Even when you don't see instant results, something begins to move in the unseen realm.

There were nights when I felt like giving up when old voices whispered that I'd never change, never be free. But in those moments, I prayed anyway. And somehow, the strength to keep going came. That's the mystery of prayer: it doesn't always remove the storm, but it gives you peace *within* it.

Prayers shift the atmosphere. When you pray, you invite the presence of God into the middle of your circumstances. Chains break. Fear loses its grip. Hope rises again. Prayers don't just change the situation, they change you.

When I prayed over my life consistently, I started to see things differently. The same challenges that once overwhelmed me became opportunities to trust God. I stopped fighting to control outcomes and started resting on His promises. Slowly, prayer began to rewire my mind, aligning my thoughts with His Word instead of my worries.

Reflection

What's one area of your life you've been trying to manage on your own strength? Take a few moments to write a simple prayer, inviting God into that specific area. Remember, your words don't have to be perfect, they just must be honest.

Here's a truth that changed me: prayer doesn't need to move mountains in a day; it just needs to move your heart a little closer to Each time. Even a whispered "Jesus, I need You" carries power when it comes from a surrendered heart.

Prayer

Lord, teach me to pray with honesty and boldness. Help me to listen for Your voice and trust that You are near. Let prayer be my first response, not my last resort. Change me from the inside out through the power of Your presence. Give me faith to keep praying even when I don't see results, and the courage to believe that You are working behind the scenes. Amen.

Verse

"Do not be anxious about anything, but in every situation, by prayer and petition, with thanksgiving, present your requests to God. And the peace of God, which transcends all understanding, will guard your hearts and your minds in Christ Jesus."

— Philippians 4:6–7 (NIV)

Chapter Five

Gratitude Changes Everything

Gratitude is one of the most powerful tools God has given us to shift our mindset. It takes our eyes off what we lack and fixes them on what we already have. When we choose gratitude, we begin to see God's fingerprints even in the ordinary moments of life.

For years, I was trapped in negativity. I focused on everything that was wrong: my mistakes, my regrets, and the things I thought I needed to be happy. I replayed failures in my mind like a broken record, convincing myself that I'd never measure up or deserve peace. But when I began to practice with gratitude, something inside me changed.

It didn't happen overnight. It started small, almost too small to notice. Instead of complaining about what I didn't have, I started thanking God for small blessings: waking up sober, a hug from my mom, the beauty of a sunrise. Gratitude didn't erase my struggles, but it gave me strength to face them with hope. Slowly, my perspective began to shift from *why me?* to *thank You, Lord, for still loving me through it all.*

Gratitude reminded me that even in my lowest moments, God was still writing a beautiful story. It opened my eyes to blessings, I had overlooked and the laughter of my child, the roof over my head, the quiet peace that comes when I finally stopped fighting for control.

Gratitude Reframes the Story

When we look at life through the lens of gratitude, we begin to see how God has been faithful all along. Even in seasons of pain, there are glimpses of His provision and care. Gratitude doesn't deny reality; it redefines it. It helps us see that what felt like a setback was often a setup for something greater.

I remember times when I prayed for something I thought I needed and God said no. Back then, I felt disappointed. But later, I realized His "no" was actually His protection. Gratitude helped me look back and recognize how He had been guiding me all along, even when I didn't understand it.

When I started to journal my blessings, I noticed patterns of grace I'd missed before. That unexpected phone call from a friend, the job that opened up at the perfect time, the peace that came during a storm and all of it was evidence that God was near.

Scripture reminds us, *"Give thanks in all circumstances; for this is God's will for you in Christ Jesus"* (1 Thessalonians 5:18, NIV). Gratitude doesn't wait for life to be perfect; it finds joy in the middle of the mess. It turns what we have into enough and transforms obstacles into opportunities for growth.

Gratitude Guards the Mind

A thankful heart leaves less room for negativity to take root. The enemy loves to whisper lies and telling you that you're behind, that you've failed, that God's forgotten you. But gratitude fights back. It's a shield that reminds you of all God has already done.

When you start each day by naming three things you're grateful for, you're training your mind to notice God's goodness. You begin to see divine details everywhere like in the sunlight filtering through your window, a song that lifts your spirit, a prayer answered in a quiet way.

Gratitude doesn't ignore pain; it gives it purpose. It reminds you that even in the valley, God is still worthy of praise. It shifts your focus from what's missing to what's eternal. His love, His mercy, His promise that He'll never leave you.

I've learned that gratitude and anxiety can't occupy the same space. When I feel worry creeping in, I stop and thank God for three things right where I am. It's amazing how quickly peace follows. Gratitude clears the fog of fear and reminds your heart that God is still in control.

As Paul wrote to the Philippians, *"Do not be anxious about anything, but in every situation, by prayer and petition, with thanksgiving, present your requests to God"* (Philippians 4:6). The "thanksgiving" part isn't a suggestion; it's a secret weapon. It's what keeps your heart anchored when life tries to pull you off course.

Gratitude Brings Joy

Joy doesn't come from having everything we want. It comes from recognizing God's presence in what we already have. Gratitude and joy are deeply connected, the more grateful you are, the more joy you experience.

Paul wrote these words from prison: *"Rejoice in the Lord always. I will say it again: Rejoice!"* (Philippians 4:4, NIV). His circumstances weren't joyful, but his heart was overflowing with gratitude. That's the paradox of faith where joy blooms in the soil of thanksgiving, even in the hardest seasons.

When I began to live from a place of gratitude, my joy returned. Not because my life became perfect, but because I started noticing the perfection of God's timing and care. Gratitude made even the simplest moments like sipping coffee on my porch or hearing my child's laughter feel sacred.

It's impossible to stay bitter when you're truly thankful. Gratitude doesn't just change your mood; it changes your posture toward life. It opens your hands instead of closing your fists. It invites peace instead of pressure.

Gratitude says, "God, I trust You even here." It's an act of worship that declares: *I may not have everything I want, but I have everything I need in You.*

A Personal Reflection

Whenever I feel disconnected from God, I remind myself of the times He met me in my darkest hours—when I felt completely lost and unworthy of love. I remember those long nights, staying up for 48 hours with friends, thinking that kind of chaos was fun. I didn't realize how much damage it was doing to my body, my mind, and my soul. But even then, God's mercy was chasing me down.

Looking back, I see how He protected me when I didn't even know I needed saving. He whispered to my heart, *"You are worthy of so much more."* And now, as I stand on the other side of that storm, I can't help but be overwhelmed with gratitude.

I'm thankful to still be here—alive, breathing, and experiencing the beauty of God's green earth. I'm thankful for my husband and our two beautiful daughters, who fill my days with laughter and purpose. I'm thankful for my parents, who never stopped praying for me, who believed that their daughter would make it through to the other side. They deserved to see me healed, whole, and walking in the light of God's grace.

That's what gratitude does it rewrites, your story. It turns your scars into testimonies and your pain into praise.

Reflection

Take a moment to write down three things you are grateful for today. They don't have to be big, start with what's right in front of you. Maybe it's your morning coffee, a friend who checks in, or simply the breath in your lungs.

Now pause and ask yourself: how does focusing on those blessings change the way you feel right now? Gratitude lifts the weight of comparison and reminds you that God's goodness is personal. It's for you, today, right where you are.

Prayer

Father, thank You for the countless blessings You've poured into my life. Teach me to live with a heart of gratitude every day. Help me to see Your goodness even in difficult seasons and let thankfulness guard my heart and mind. When negativity tries to steal my joy, remind me of all the ways You've been faithful. May gratitude be my default, not my afterthought. Amen.

Verse

"Give thanks in all circumstances; for this is God's will for you in Christ Jesus."

— 1 Thessalonians 5:18 (NIV)

Chapter Six

Speaking Life Over Yourself

The words we speak hold incredible power. Proverbs reminds us, *"The tongue has the power of life and death, and those who love it will eat its fruit"* (Proverbs 18:21, NIV). What we say about ourselves can either build us up or tear us down. Too often, we repeat the lies of the enemy out loud, reinforcing his deception instead of declaring God's truth.

For many years, I didn't realize how harsh my own words toward myself had become. I would say things like, *"I'll never get it right,"* or *"I'm such a failure."* Those words weren't harmless; they were agreements with the enemy's lies. Every time I spoke them, I was feeding negativity and giving it permission to grow. It wasn't until I began intentionally speaking God's truth over my life that I saw real change in my mindset and my future.

Life or Death in the Tongue

Your words are seeds. When you speak life, you plant hope, faith, and courage in your heart. When you speak death, you plant doubt, fear, and despair. Think about the words you've spoken recently. Are they in agreement with God's Word, or are they in agreement with the enemy's lies?

We live in a world that normalizes self-criticism. People casually say, *"I'm so dumb,"* or *"I could never do that,"* without realizing they're cursing the very potential God placed within them. Every word you speak shapes the atmosphere around you and your home, your heart, and even your destiny.

When I began to change the way I talked to myself, my world changed with it. The moment I stopped saying, *"I can't,"* and began saying, *"With God's help, I can,"* I noticed a shift not only in my attitude but in the way I showed up each day. God's Word doesn't just challenge us to think differently — it invites us to speak differently. The language of faith creates life where there once was despair.

Declaring God's Truth

One of the most effective ways to renew your mind is to declare Scripture out loud. When you proclaim what God says about you, you are actively resisting the enemy. Speaking God's truth builds faith, even when your feelings haven't caught up yet.

Instead of saying, *"I am weak,"* declare, *"The Lord is my strength and my shield"* (Psalm 28:7, NIV).

Instead of saying, *"I can't change,"* declare, *"I can do all this through him who gives me strength"* (Philippians 4:13, NIV).

Instead of saying, *"I am not enough,"* declare, *"I am fearfully and wonderfully made"* (Psalm 139:14, NIV).

When you speak the Word, you shift the atmosphere around you. Heaven listens when you declare truth, and the enemy trembles when you proclaim God's promises. There's something powerful about hearing your own voice declare life and it reprograms your spirit to believe what God says instead of what the world or your past has told you.

Changing Your Inner Dialogue

The way you talk to yourself shapes how you live. If your inner dialogue is constantly critical, you will struggle to believe the truth. But if you learn to align your self-talk with God's Word, you will begin to walk in freedom. Speaking life over yourself is not about ignoring reality; it's about declaring God's reality over your circumstances.

There were days when I'd wake up already defeated, but before I even got out of bed. I'd look in the mirror and see every flaw, every failure, every reason I thought I wasn't enough. But one morning, God convicted my heart. He whispered, *"Stop speaking death over what I have called good."*

That changed everything. I began to intentionally reframe my words. Instead of saying, *"I'm exhausted,"* I said, *"God is renewing my strength."* Instead of, *"I'm overwhelmed,"* I declared, *"God's peace is guarding my heart and mind."* It didn't mean I stopped feeling tired or stressed, it meant I chose faith over fear in my speech.

This practice doesn't happen overnight. It's a daily habit and a discipline of the tongue and the mind. When you catch yourself speaking negatively, pause. Replace that thought with a declaration of truth. Over time, your words will align with your faith, and your faith will reshape your reality.

The Battle Over Your Words

The enemy knows the power of your words — that's why he attacks them. If he can control your tongue, he can control your mindset. Remember, his strategy has always been to twist truth into deception. He doesn't need to destroy you outright; he just needs you to agree with the wrong things long enough for you to stop walking in your authority.

When Jesus was tempted in the wilderness, He didn't stay silent. He fought back with the Word of God. Every time Satan tried to lie to Him, Jesus replied, *"It is written."* That's the same authority you have. When the enemy whispers, *"You're not forgiven,"* you respond, *"It is written — there is no condemnation for those who are in Christ Jesus"* (Romans 8:1). When he says, *"You're too far gone,"* you declare, *"It is written — God's mercy is new every morning"* (Lamentations 3:22–23).

Your tongue can be a weapon of warfare. Use it to defend your peace, your purpose, and your promise.

Practical Steps to Speak Life

- Write down five scriptures that remind you of your identity in Christ.
- Each morning, read them out loud as declarations over your life even when you don't feel it.
- Replace lies with truth immediately when negative thoughts creep in.
- Record your declarations on your phone and play them back during your morning drive or workout.

- Surround yourself with voices that speak life like solid friends, sermons, and even songs that echo God's truth.

When you make speaking life a daily practice, it becomes part of who you are. You begin to live out the reality of what you've been declaring all along.

A Personal Reflection

There were seasons when my own words were my biggest enemy. I didn't need anyone else to tear me down because I was already doing it myself. I remember sitting in my car after a tough day, feeling like I'd failed as a mom, a wife, and a believer. Tears filled my eyes, and before I could even pray, the Holy Spirit whispered, *"Would you talk to your daughter the way you talk to yourself?"*

That question wrecked me. Of course, I wouldn't. I would never tell her she wasn't enough or that she'd never change. I would speak life over her, remind her who she is, and tell her how deeply loved she is by God. And in that moment, I realized that's exactly how God wants me to speak to myself.

From then on, I made a promise to start talking to myself the way my Heavenly Father talks to me with compassion, patience, and truth. Now, when I catch myself saying something harsh, I pause and replace it with His words: *"You are chosen. You are loved. You are forgiven. You are growing."*

Reflection

What words have you been speaking over yourself lately? Are they words of life or words of death? Write down a negative phrase you often say about yourself and then write the truth from Scripture to replace it. You might be surprised by how quickly your spirit lifts when you begin to speak God's truth instead of your fears.

Remember, your words are not just sounds. They are seeds that will eventually bear fruit. Choose to plant life.

Prayer

Father, forgive me for the times I've spoken death over my life instead of life. Teach me to use my words to align with Your truth. Help me to speak encouragement, faith, and hope over myself and others. Let every word that leaves my mouth bring life, not destruction. When I'm tempted to agree with the enemy's lies, remind me that Your Word is the final authority. In Jesus' name, amen.

Verse

"The tongue has the power of life and death,
and those who love it will eat its fruit."

— Proverbs 18:21 (NIV)

Chapter Seven

Finding Strength in Weakness

Weakness isn't something most of us like to admit. We live in a world that glorifies strength, independence, and self-sufficiency. But God's kingdom works differently. In His upside-down way of doing things, it's often in our weakest moments that His power shines the brightest.

For years, I thought weakness meant failure. I believed that if I admitted my struggles, people would see me as *less than,* or that God would be disappointed in me. But the truth is, weakness is the doorway to God's strength. The Apostle Paul wrote, *"But he said to me, 'My grace is sufficient for you, for my power is made perfect in weakness.' Therefore, I will boast even more gladly about my weaknesses, so that Christ's power may rest on me"* (2 Corinthians 12:9, NIV).

Learning to Depend on God

My old life was built on pride and self-reliance. I thought I could handle everything on my own, until I couldn't. Substance abuse exposed how fragile my strength really was. No matter how hard I tried, I couldn't break free by myself. My own willpower always ran out. It was only when I admitted my weakness and cried out to God that His strength carried me through.

In those early days of surrender, I felt like I was falling apart, but God was rebuilding me from the inside out. I remember kneeling beside my bed, trembling, tears soaking the pillow as I whispered, *"God, I can't do this anymore."* That confession wasn't defeat; it was the beginning of freedom. Heaven rushed in the moment I let go of the illusion of control.

Weakness isn't a liability in God's eyes; it's an opportunity. When we stop pretending, we have it all together, we create space for God's grace to flow. His power isn't attracted to our perfection; it's drawn to our humility.

So many of us are walking around exhausted because we're trying to be our own savior. We fix, we strive, we hide, but the real strength comes when we finally say, *"Lord, I need You."*

God's Power Made Perfect

We often pray for God to take away our struggles, but sometimes He allows them to remain so we can learn to lean on Him. Paul pleaded with God three times to remove his "thorn in the flesh," but God responded with those life-changing words: *"My grace is sufficient for you."*

That means God's grace isn't just *enough*. It's *more than enough*. His strength doesn't show up *despite* your weakness, but right in the middle of it.

There have been times when I begged God to take away my battles and the anxiety, the fear of failure, the reminders of my past. But repeatedly, He whispered, *"My grace is enough for this too."* And somehow, even when I didn't feel strong, I was still standing. That's what grace does, it carries you when your legs can't.

Sometimes we misunderstand what strength really is. We think it's about never falling apart, but true strength is trusting that even when you do, God can rebuild what's broken. His power rests not on the person who appears to have it together, but on the one humble enough to admit, *"I don't, but God does."*

The Gift Hidden in Weakness

If we never struggled, we'd never need grace. If we never felt weak, we'd never know the depth of God's strength. Our weaknesses aren't punishment; they're the soil where His power grows.

Looking back, some of my weakest moments became my greatest teachers. When I was too tired to pray, too ashamed to hope, God met me there. He didn't wait for me to clean myself up or find perfect words. He just showed up in the middle of my mess and held me steadily.

I can see now that the nights I spent crying out to Him weren't wasted. They were sacred. Those were the moments He was refining me, teaching me that I didn't need to prove my worth. I just needed to receive His grace.

If you've ever felt like your weakness disqualifies you, remember this: it's the very thing God can use to qualify you. He doesn't choose the strong; He strengthens the chosen.

Redefining Strength

The world says strength is about control, power, and never showing vulnerability. God says true strength is found in surrender, humility, and dependence on Him. When we try to carry life on our own, we eventually collapse. When we let God carry us, we find endurance we never thought possible.

I used to measure strength by how much I could endure without crying or asking for help. I thought holding it together made me powerful. But strength without surrender only breeds pride. Real power is saying, *"God, I can't, but You can."*

There's beauty in brokenness when it's placed in God's hands. Like clay in the potter's palm, our cracks become the very places His light shines through. The same God who formed the stars isn't intimidated by your struggles. He delights in taking what's weak and making it radiant with His power.

When I look back on my journey, I realize that every breakdown became a breakthrough. Every season that humbled me also healed me. I stopped asking, *"Why is this happening to me?"* and started saying, *"God, what are You strengthening in me through this?"*

The Strength That Stays

God's strength doesn't fade when the spotlight moves away. It's not loud or boastful, it's quiet, steady, and faithful. It's the kind of strength that helps you show up one more day, loved one more time, and hope one more time even after disappointment.

You might not feel strong right now, but feelings aren't the foundation of your faith. And the truth is this: the same power that raised Jesus from the dead lives in you (Romans 8:11).

When you're weak, that power activates. It's not your grit keeping you going; it's His grace. Every morning you choose to rise, you're walking proof that God's strength is alive and well within you.

A Personal Reflection

There was a season when weakness felt like my identity. My body was tired, my spirit was heavy, and I felt like I was failing in every area. I remember looking in the mirror and saying out loud, *"I don't even recognize who I am anymore."*

That day, God met me in my reflection. Not in a booming voice, but in a quiet, loving whisper: *"You are still Mine."* Tears fell as I realized I didn't have to earn His strength was already available.

I learned to stop running from the weak parts of me and start inviting God into them. The parts I once hid in shame became the very areas He used to show His glory. When I share my story now, it's not from a place of shame, but victory. Because every weakness surrendered to God becomes a testimony of His power.

Today, I no longer see weakness as failure. I see it as a holy invitation, but an open door where my strength ends and His begins.

Practical Steps to Embrace Strength Through Weakness

1. Admit it honestly. Stop pretending you have it all together. Bring your weaknesses into the light through prayer or journaling. God can only heal what you reveal.
2. Ask for help. Whether from God or from trusted people, humility opens the door to support. You were never meant to carry life alone.
3. Speak grace over yourself. When you fail or fall short, declare, "His grace is sufficient for me."
4. Look for lessons, not losses. Every struggle carries a lesson about dependence, trust, or patience.
5. Rest in God's timing. His strength often arrives in small, quiet ways through rest, peace, or unexpected encouragement.

Reflection

What weakness in your life have you been trying to hide or fix on your own? Write it down. Then ask God to show you how His strength can be made perfect in that area.

Spend a few moments thanking Him for the times He carried you when you didn't even realize it. Let gratitude turn your weakness into worship.

Prayer

Lord, I confess my weakness to You. I don't want to pretend I have it all together anymore. Fill me with Your grace and power so that others may see You at work in me. Teach me to depend on You daily. Help me remember that my limitations are not a curse, they're an invitation to experience Your strength. When I feel like giving up, remind me that You are my refuge and my portion forever. Thank You for meeting me in my weakness and turning it into a testimony of Your faithfulness. Amen.

Verse

"But he said to me, 'My grace is sufficient for you, for my power is made perfect in weakness.' Therefore, I will boast more gladly about my weaknesses, so that Christ's power may rest on me."

— 2 Corinthians 12:9 (NIV)

Chapter Eight

Guarding Your Heart

Your heart is the wellspring of your life. Proverbs 4:23 (NIV) says, *"Above all else, guard your heart, for everything you do flows from it."* The condition of your heart determines the direction of your life. If your heart is filled with bitterness, fear, or resentment, it will shape your thoughts, words, and actions. But when your heart is rooted in God's truth and love, you will live from a place of peace and strength.

For years, I let everything into my heart. I didn't filter the voices I listened to or the influences I allowed around me. Toxic relationships, destructive habits, and negative environments all left their mark. My heart was unguarded, and it showed. I carried wounds, insecurities, and anger that spilled out in the way I lived. It wasn't until I surrendered my heart to God that I began to understand what it meant to truly guard it.

The Heart Is the Source

Everything in life flows from the heart… your joy, your peace, your words, your choices. The heart is where faith is planted and where doubt tries to take root.

That's why the enemy attacks it first. If he can contaminate your heart with lies, he can redirect your whole life.

When your heart is heavy, it colors the way you see the world. I remember seasons when my heart was clouded with anger and disappointment. I'd wake up already defensive, ready to protect myself from more pain. But I wasn't protecting my heart, I was building walls out of fear.

God doesn't ask us to harden our hearts; He asks us to guard them. There's a difference. Hardness shuts people out. Guarding keeps truth in and deception out.

When you let God be the keeper of your heart, peace becomes your protection. His Spirit begins to filter what enters — the words you hear, the things you watch, the emotions you dwell on. What used to break you begins to strengthen you.

Setting Boundaries

Guarding your heart doesn't mean shutting people out or building walls; it means setting healthy boundaries. Not every voice deserves access to your soul. Some people will drain you, discourage you, or pull you away from God's purpose. Loving them doesn't mean giving them permission to shape your identity.

There was a time I thought setting boundaries meant I wasn't being kind or Christian enough. I confused meekness with weakness. I kept saying yes when God was telling me to say no. The result? I was spiritually exhausted and emotionally empty.

When I finally learned that guarding my heart was obedience, everything changed. I began to pray, *"Lord, show me who's meant to walk with me and who's meant to be loved from a distance."* That prayer saved me from countless heartbreaks and helped me focus on the relationships that truly bore fruit.

Guarding your heart isn't about isolation; it's about discernment. Even Jesus withdrew to quiet places to pray and reset His heart. He loved everyone, but He wasn't always accessible to everyone. That's wisdom.

Ask yourself: *Who or what am I giving too much access to my heart?* If it doesn't draw you closer to God, it might be time to draw a boundary.

Feeding Your Heart Truth

Your heart will always be shaped by whatever you feed it. If you constantly take in negativity, comparison, or lies from the world, that's what will grow inside you. But if you fill your heart with God's Word, prayer, and worship, you'll be strengthened from the inside out.

Jesus said, *"A good man brings good things out of the good stored up in him"* (Matthew 12:35, NIV). So what are you storing in your heart?

When I began to replace noise with worship, something beautiful happened. Peace started to take root where chaos once lived. I used to wake up and scroll social media, comparing my life to others. It always left me feeling "less than." But when I started my mornings in Scripture, I noticed a new calm in my spirit. The things that used to trigger insecurity no longer had the same power.

What you feed will grow. Feed your heart with truth and lies will lose their appetite.

Healing for the Broken Heart

Many of us carry wounds from the past like disappointments, betrayals, and losses that left cracks in our hearts. Guarding your heart also means letting God heal those broken places. If we don't, bitterness and pain become filters through which we see the world.

There was a time when I said I'd forgiven someone, but deep down, I hadn't. Every time their name came up, my stomach turned. I realized that although my lips said "I forgive," my heart was still chained to resentment. God had to show me that guarding my heart wasn't about building a fortress; it was about inviting Him to cleanse it.

Psalm 147:3 (NIV) promises, *"He heals the brokenhearted and binds up their wounds."* That's not a metaphor, it's a promise. God doesn't just patch your heart; He restores it. He takes the shattered pieces and creates something stronger and softer all at once.

If your heart feels broken beyond repair, know this: God specializes in restoration. He has never met a wound He couldn't heal.

Letting Go of Emotional Clutter

Sometimes guarding your heart means decluttering it. Over time, we collect emotional baggage, old memories, grudges, words spoken over us that still sting. We hold on to these things, not realizing they're poisoning the wellspring of life within us.

Think of your heart like a garden. When weeds grow unchecked, they choke out the beauty. Guarding your heart means allowing the Gardener God Himself to pull up the weeds. Some of those weeds might be relationships that no longer serve your growth, habits that dull your spirit, or thoughts that keep you bound.

You can't experience peace while you're nurturing pain. Sometimes healing begins when you simply say, *"Lord, take this from me. I'm tired of watering what's meant to die."*

God's Peace as a Guard

Philippians 4:7 says, *"And the peace of God, which transcends all understanding, will guard your hearts and your minds in Christ Jesus."*

Peace is more than a feeling; it's a fortress. When your heart is surrendered to God, His peace becomes a shield against anxiety, fear, and offense.

You'll know your heart is guarded when you no longer react the same way to things that once triggered you. You stop chasing validation and start resting in your identity. You stop carrying burdens that were never yours to hold.

Peace doesn't mean life gets easy, it means your spirit stays steady even when the storm rages.

A Personal Reflection

There was a time when my heart was wide open but unprotected. I thought being open-hearted meant saying yes to everyone and everything. I let people speak into my life who had no business holding that kind of authority over my soul. The result was confusion, pain, and spiritual exhaustion.

When I finally handed my heart to God, He began to teach me discernment. He showed me how to recognize His voice from all the noise. He helped me see that not everyone who smiles has pure intentions, and not every opportunity is from Him.

Now, I ask God daily to help me guard my heart not from love, but from anything that would contaminate it. I've learned that peace is priceless and protecting it is part of walking in wisdom.

There's such freedom in realizing you can love deeply and still have boundaries. You can forgive fully and still protect your peace. You can walk in grace without being a doormat.

Guarding your heart doesn't make you cold; it keeps you capable of loving the right way with discernment, grace, and truth.

Practical Steps to Guard Your Heart

1. Start your day with God. Before you open your phone, open your Bible. Fill your heart with truth before the world has a chance to fill it with noise.
2. Limit access. Not everyone should have a front-row seat to your emotions. Pray about who belongs in your inner circle.
3. Forgive quickly. Don't give offense a place to live. Forgiveness doesn't excuse behavior it frees your heart.
4. Stay watchful. Pay attention to what triggers unrest. Sometimes the Holy Spirit is nudging you to guard your peace.
5. Speak life. Your words shape your heart. Declare over yourself: *"My heart is anchored in Christ. My peace is protected. My joy is secure."*

Reflection

What influences have you been allowing into your heart lately? Are they drawing you closer to God or pulling you away? Write down one boundary you need to set and one way you can begin feeding your heart with God's truth.

Take a moment to ask yourself: *What would my life look like if my heart were fully guarded by peace instead of fear?*

Prayer

Father, I give You my heart today. Guard it from the lies of the enemy and the distractions of the world. Heal the wounds I still carry and fill me with Your truth and love so that everything I do flows from a heart surrendered to You. Help me recognize what needs to stay and what needs to go. Teach me to love with discernment and to rest in Your peace. Thank You for being the ultimate protector of my heart. Amen.

Verse

"Above all else, guard your heart,
for everything you do flows from it."

— Proverbs 4:23 (NIV)

Chapter Nine

RENEWING YOUR MIND DAILY

Renewing your mind is not a one-time event; it's a daily choice. Romans 12:2 (NIV) says, *"Do not conform to the pattern of this world, but be transformed by the renewing of your mind. Then you will be able to test and approve what God's will is his good, pleasing and perfect will."* Transformation doesn't happen in a single moment; it's a process we walk out each day with God.

Early in my journey, I thought going to church once a week would be enough to change me. But by Monday morning, I was right back in my old mindset. I quickly realized that just as my body needs food daily, my spirit and mind need to be fed daily with God's truth. Renewing your mind means choosing each day to align your thoughts with God's Word instead of the world's lies.

Why Renewal Must Be Daily

Your mind is a battlefield, and every day brings a new fight for your focus. The world shouts its opinions louder than ever through screens, headlines, and even your own inner critic. If you don't intentionally renew your mind, negativity will slowly take over.

Renewing your mind is more than positive thinking; it's spiritual alignment. It's waking up and deciding: *Today, I will believe what God says about me, not what fear says about me.*

When you renew your mind, you reset your direction. You allow the Holy Spirit to wash away yesterday's worries and refresh your thoughts for today's assignments. The same way you shower to remove dirt from your body, you must wash your mind daily with the Word to remove doubt, guilt, and lies that try to cling to you.

Start with Scripture

The Bible is the foundation of a renewed mind. When you read even a few verses a day, you're planting seeds of truth that push back against the lies of the enemy. Don't feel pressured to read chapters at a time. Start small and let God speak to you through His Word. A single verse can carry you through an entire day.

Some mornings I read only one line before chaos begins maybe a verse scribbled on a sticky note near my coffee cup. Yet that one verse has often anchored me through storms. God's Word is alive; it breathes strength into weary places.

You don't have to read to impress God, you read to invite Him in. Think of Scripture as daily nourishment: it may feel small in the moment, but over time it changes everything.

Try reading aloud. Let your own ears hear truth. When your thoughts begin to spiral later in the day, that verse will echo back, steadying you when life shakes.

Practice Consistency

Consistency is more powerful than intensity. Spending fifteen minutes with God every day will transform you far more than spending two hours once a month. The enemy wants you to believe you're too busy, but the truth is, you can't afford *not* to renew your mind daily.

Think of your mind like a garden. If you neglect it, weeds of anxiety and distraction quickly take over. But daily care even small doses keep it thriving.

There were seasons when my schedule was chaos kids, work, deadlines, exhaustion and my time with God felt almost impossible. But I started turning small moments into holy ones: worship music while washing dishes, a quick prayer in the car line, reading one Psalm before bed. God met me there. He doesn't need hours of perfection; He wants moments of presence.

Over time, those small daily choices built unshakable faith. It wasn't about grand gestures; it was about steady surrender.

Replace Lies with Truth

Negative thoughts don't disappear on their own; you must replace them with truth. Every lie believed must be evicted by a greater truth.

When you face discouragement, declare God's promises out loud. When you feel unworthy, remind yourself that you are chosen and loved. Over time, these truths reshape how you think and live.

I used to replay mistakes in my mind like a highlight reel of shame. Every time I'd start something new, those old failures whispered, *You'll mess this up too.* One day, I decided to fight back. I wrote down Scriptures that directly contradicted those lies and verses about grace, purpose, and renewal. Then, whenever a negative thought crept in, I spoke God's Word instead. Slowly but surely, the lies lost their power.

The enemy cannot stand against truth spoken with faith. When your thoughts begin to spiral, pause and ask, *Is this from God or from fear?* If it's not from God, replace it immediately.

Think Higher, Live Freer

The renewal of your mind isn't just about thinking better, it's about living freer. As your thoughts change, your actions follow.

You begin to see yourself as God sees you as capable, loved, redeemed, and equipped. You start to approach challenges with faith instead of fear. The things that used to paralyze you become platforms for God's glory.

Renewing your mind shifts you from reaction to reflection. Instead of letting emotions rule, you begin to respond with wisdom. The more you meditate on truth, the more peace governs your heart.

Isaiah 26:3 (NIV) says, *"You will keep in perfect peace those whose minds are steadfast, because they trust in you."* Peace is the fruit of a renewed mind.

Renewal in the Mundane

Renewing your mind isn't reserved for Sunday mornings or mountaintop moments. It happens in ordinary spaces in traffic, during laundry, while rocking a baby back to sleep.

Every time you choose gratitude over grumbling, patience over panic, faith over fear you renew your mind. The more you practice it, the more natural it becomes.

You don't have to wait for perfect quiet to connect with God. He meets you in motion. Whisper prayers while you walk. Turn worship music into your background soundtrack. Let your environment remind you of His presence until renewal becomes your rhythm.

A Personal Reflection

There was a time when my thoughts ruled me instead of the other way around. I'd wake up anxious, replaying mistakes and worrying about what might go wrong. My mind was loud with fear.

But one morning, sitting on my porch with a cup of coffee and my Bible open to Romans 12:2, something clicked: transformation isn't a single miracle; it's a daily partnership. God renews, but I must invite Him to.

So, I began my "five-minute rule." No matter how busy I was, I'd give God the first five minutes of my morning. Some days it was worship; others it was reading one verse or just sitting in silence. But those five minutes became sacred ground. They grew into ten, then twenty, until spending time with God became my favorite part of the day.

Renewal became my lifestyle, not my checklist. I still have hard days, but now I know where to run when my thoughts wander.

Practical Steps to Renew Your Mind

1. Morning Truths: Read or listen to one Scripture before you check your phone.
2. Speak It Out: Declare one positive, Bible-based affirmation daily (e.g., "*I have the mind of Christ.*").
3. Create a Truth List: Write down lies you often believe, then find a verse that replaces each one.

4. Set a Reminder: Schedule a midday pause to reset, breathe, pray, and realign your focus.
5. Nightly Reflection: Before bed, thank God for one truth you lived out that day.

Little moments, repeated faithfully, build lasting transformation.

Reflection

What's one small habit you can start today to renew your mind daily? Write it down and commit to practicing it for the next week. Then notice how your thoughts begin to shift — not overnight, but steadily, like dawn breaking after a long night.

Prayer

Lord, teach me to renew my mind every day with Your truth. Give me discipline to spend time in Your Word and courage to reject the lies of the enemy. Transform me day by day so that I may live in Your perfect will. When distractions come, help me return to You quickly. When I feel weary, remind me that Your Word refreshes my soul. Let my thoughts bring You glory, and my life reflect Your peace. Amen.

Verse

"Do not conform to the pattern of this world but be transformed by the renewing of your mind. Then you will be able to test and approve what God's will is his good, pleasing and perfect will."

— Romans 12:2 (NIV)

4. Set a Reminder: [illegible] a mid-day pause to reset [illegible] [illegible]

5. Mid-day Reflection Pause: [illegible] God [illegible] you lived [illegible]

[illegible]

Reflection

[illegible]

[illegible]

[illegible]

Chapter Ten

WALKING IN FREEDOM

Freedom in Christ is not just a concept; it's a way of life. Galatians 5:1 (NIV) declares, *"It is for freedom that Christ has set us free. Stand firm, then, and do not let yourselves be burdened again by a yoke of slavery."*

When Jesus saves us, He doesn't just forgive our sins; He breaks the chains that once held us captive and invites us into a life of lasting freedom.

For years, I didn't understand what real freedom was. I thought freedom meant doing whatever I wanted, whenever I wanted. But that path led only to bondage and then to addiction, shame, and emptiness. Real freedom came when I surrendered my life to Jesus. Only then did I discover that freedom isn't found in living without rules; it's found in living under God's grace and truth.

The Illusion of Freedom

The world tells us freedom means control to say yes to every desire, to chase every thrill. But what the world calls freedom often leads to slavery. My "yes" became a trap: one more night out, one more drink, one more pill to numb what I didn't want to face. I was chasing happiness and losing myself in the process.

I remember the exhaustion of living that way the constant pretending, the broken promises to myself, the ache of waking up wondering why I was still here. I thought I was free because no one could tell me what to do. In reality, I was chained to choices that were destroying me.

That's the thing about sin: it advertises pleasure but delivers pain. What begins as escape becomes imprisonment. I didn't realize that real freedom doesn't mean living without boundaries; it means living within God's love where peace, purpose, and safety exist.

A Wake-Up Call at 21 Years Old

At just 21 years old, my choices finally caught up to me. I was rushed into surgery to have my gallbladder removed. It's a procedure people twice my age were having, not someone barely old enough to drink legally. My body was breaking down from the inside out.

Years of binge drinking had already left a mark. I had treated my body like it was disposable, never realizing how much damage I was doing. I remember lying in that hospital bed, fluorescent lights flickering above me, thinking, *This isn't how my story is supposed to go.*

I wasn't just physically sick; I was spiritually empty. The surgery itself wasn't what scared me most, it was the realization that I had come so close to losing everything. I could feel God's whisper in that sterile hospital room, cutting through the noise: *"You're still Mine. I'm not done with you yet."*

Even then, when addiction tried to take me down when Satan wanted to end my story early, God stepped in. He protected me even when I wasn't looking for Him. That hospital stay became the line in the sand. Something inside me shifted. I didn't change overnight, but I knew deep down: I was meant for more.

Breaking the Chains

Addiction had become my identity. It promised relief and destruction. I used to think no one could understand the grip it had on me, the way it stole my peace and numbed my purpose. But God did. And He didn't wait for me to clean up first; He met me right where I was.

Freedom started the moment I stopped pretending I could do it on my own. I cried out to God with the same broken voice I'd once used to curse Him. And instead of condemnation, I felt compassion. He didn't scold me for falling, He helped me stand.

It's been almost ten years now, and every sober day feels like a miracle. The cravings that once ruled my life have been replaced with clarity and gratitude. My mind is clear, my spirit is strong, and my heart is alive. Every time I look back, I see God's fingerprints on the pages of my recovery, proof that His mercy is greater than any mistake.

The enemy tried to destroy me, but God rewrote my story. The same hands that once reached for pills now reach for purpose. The same voice that once spoke shame now speaks life.

Freedom from the Past

One of the enemy's favorite strategies is to keep you chained to your past. He whispers reminders of your failures, hoping you'll believe you'll never change. But God's Word says, *"Therefore, if anyone is in Christ, the new creation has come: The old has gone, the new is here!"* (2 Corinthians 5:17, NIV). When God sets you free, your past no longer defines you.

I've learned that freedom doesn't mean forgetting the past, it means no longer being bound by it. My scars are reminders, not shackles. They tell the story of a Savior who rescued me when I couldn't rescue myself.

Sometimes the most powerful testimony isn't perfection, it's redemption. When people see the joy I walk in now, they don't see the mess I came from, but I will always remember. And that's what makes me grateful.

Freedom in Your Identity

True freedom comes when you know who you are in Christ. You are no longer a slave to sin but a child of God. When you believe this truth, the lies of the enemy lose their grip. Walking in freedom means choosing every day to live from your God-given identity, not the labels the world tries to put on you.

For so long, I labeled myself as "broken," "addict," "failure." But God renamed me: *healed, redeemed, chosen.* Once you understand your identity in Him, you stop seeking validation from the places that hurt you.

Freedom doesn't mean you'll never face temptation again; it means temptation no longer has authority over you. The chains are gone, but you still must choose to walk out of the prison door every day.

Freedom to Live with Purpose

God doesn't set us free just for ourselves. He sets us free so we can help set others free. Your story of redemption is a testimony that can bring hope to those still trapped.

When I share what God has done, I'm not glorifying the pain, I'm magnifying the One who healed it. I've had people message me saying, *"If you can come out of that, maybe I can too."* That's the power of walking in freedom. It's contagious.

We were never meant to hoard our healing; it's meant to overflow. God can take your darkest season and use it to light someone else's path.

A Personal Reflection

Sometimes I think back to that 21-year-old girl in the hospital bed who was scared, empty, and unsure if life would ever get better. I wish I could tell her that one day she'd be free, free from addiction, free from shame, free from the lies that once ruled her mind.

I wish she knew that one day she'd wake up clear-minded and full of purpose. That the same girl who once chased escape would now chase God's presence. That her story would become a message of hope.

Ten years later, I can say with certainty: God never wastes a wilderness. The very things that broke me became the foundation of my faith. Freedom isn't about never struggling; it's about knowing who holds you through every struggle.

If you're reading this and wondering if true freedom is possible for you, it is. The chains you feel are real, but so is the God who can break them. You are meant for so much more than the pain you've been through.

Practical Steps to Walk in Freedom

1. Stay connected to God. Freedom requires daily fellowship with the One who sets you free. Prayer and worship are lifelines.
2. Replace triggers with truth. Identify what tempts you and combat it with Scripture.

3. Surround yourself with support. Freedom flourishes in community, not isolation.
4. Keep your testimony alive. Share what God has done, it strengthens you and inspires others.
5. Stay grateful. Gratitude keeps your focus on how far God has brought you, not how far you still have to go.

Reflection

Where have you been living as though you are still in chains, even though Christ has already set you free? Write down one area where you need to fully embrace your freedom in Him.

Then, take a moment to thank God for what He's already delivered you from because you're not who you used to be.

Prayer

Lord, thank You for the freedom You purchased for me on the cross. Thank You for rescuing me when I couldn't rescue myself. Teach me to walk boldly in that freedom every day. Help me to let go of the lies of the past and live fully as the new creation You have made me. Use my story to bring hope to others who feel trapped. May my life be proof that no one is too far gone for Your grace. Amen.

Verse

"It is for freedom that Christ has set us free. Stand firm, then, and do not let yourselves be burdened again by a yoke of slavery."

— Galatians 5:1 (NIV)

Chapter Eleven

LIVING WITH PURPOSE

God did not create you by accident. Every life has a purpose, and yours is no exception. Ephesians 2:10 (NIV) says, *"For we are God's handiwork, created in Christ Jesus to do good works, which God prepared in advance for us to do."*

Living with purpose means aligning your life with God's plan and using your gifts to make a difference in the world.

For many years, I wandered through life without direction. I thought my purpose was to chase pleasure and avoid pain. But that way of living left me empty and broken. When I gave my life to Christ, He showed me that my true purpose was not about serving myself but about serving Him and others. Purpose is not found in possessions, status, or success it is found in walking daily with Jesus.

From Wandering to Walking

There's a difference between movement and direction. I used to mistake one for the other. I was constantly moving and chasing jobs, relationships, validation, and moments of temporary joy, yet I wasn't going anywhere meaningful. My life felt like a treadmill: exhausting motion with no progress.

When I finally stopped long enough to ask God, *"Why am I here?"* He didn't answer with a career title or a five-year plan. He answered with peace. He whispered, *"You're here to know Me, love Me, and make My love known."*

That realization changed everything. Purpose wasn't something I had to chase; it was something I had to uncover by walking with Him.

When you invite God into your daily life, you begin to see how everything, even your mistakes and your pain can serve a purpose. The same broken road that once led me to destruction now leads me to help others find healing.

Discovering Your God-Given Purpose

God has placed unique gifts and talents inside each of us. Living with purpose means asking Him how to use those gifts for His glory. Your purpose doesn't have to be something grand in the eyes of the world. Sometimes it's as simple as showing kindness, raising your family in faith, or encouraging someone who is struggling.

When you surrender your gifts to God, He multiplies them in ways you could never imagine.

I used to think purpose had to be something dramatic like starting a ministry, speaking on stages, or writing books. But purpose is just as powerful in the quiet moments: listening to a friend in pain, praying for a stranger, or teaching your children to love Jesus.

God uses ordinary people to do extraordinary things when they simply say yes. You don't have to be perfect, polished, or qualified. You just need to be willing.

When you begin to see your daily life as sacred, purpose becomes your lifestyle, not a destination.

Purpose Through Service

One of the greatest ways to step into your purpose is to serve others. Jesus modeled this perfectly when He washed the feet of His disciples. Living with purpose often looks like humility, compassion, and love in action.

When you serve others, you reflect Christ and experience fulfillment that nothing else can give.

There's something holy about serving that takes your eyes off yourself and places them on others. Whether it's volunteering, mentoring, or simply offering a listening ear, every act of service builds the Kingdom of God.

When I began serving in children's ministry, I didn't realize how deeply it would impact me. Watching little faces light up when they learned about Jesus reminded me of my own journey and how God met me when I was broken and began shaping me for something greater. Service doesn't just change others; it changes you.

Purpose grows stronger every time you give without expecting anything in return.

Overcoming Distractions

The enemy will do everything he can to keep you from living with purpose. He'll distract you with busyness, comparison, or feelings of inadequacy. He doesn't have to destroy you; he just has to keep you distracted long enough to delay your destiny.

I know that struggle well. There were times I felt like I was making progress, only to get pulled back into old habits of doubt. I'd look at other people's lives and think, *"They're doing so much more than me."* But God reminded me that comparison kills contentment. He has a plan for each of us perfectly timed, perfectly tailored.

Proverbs 19:21 (NIV) reminds us, *"Many are the plans in a person's heart, but it is the Lord's purpose that prevails."*

When you feel lost or discouraged, remember that even delays have divine purpose. Sometimes God slows us down to strengthen us. Sometimes He closes doors not to punish us, but to protect us.

Living with purpose doesn't mean you'll always understand what God is doing, it means you trust Him anyway.

Purpose Is Found in the Process

One of the hardest lessons I've learned is that purpose isn't always revealed in a single moment, it unfolds through seasons. Every season, even the painful ones, prepares you for the next.

I can look back now and see how every struggle from addiction to recovery, from fear to faith, was part of the process. God used it all to build endurance, empathy, and faith.

Sometimes the very thing you're asking God to take away is the tool He's using to shape your purpose. The storm that almost destroyed you becomes the testimony that frees someone else.

When you understand that, you stop resenting the process and start respecting it.

A Personal Reflection

There was a time when I believed I had no purpose. I had made too many mistakes, burned too many bridges, and truly thought God had given up on me. But now I see that the years I once considered wasted were years of preparation shaping me, humbling me, and drawing me back to Him.

For a season, I was singing on the worship team at my church. Using my voice to glorify God became one of the sweetest parts of my life. But I ignored the signs. I pushed through vocal strain, overlooked the pain, and carried vocal nodules far longer than I should have. Eventually, I had to step back and maybe even bring that chapter of my singing journey to a close.

It has been painful, not just physically, but emotionally too. Losing the ability to sing the way I once did felt like losing a piece of who I am. But even in this, God has been faithful. I am constantly healing, learning new ways to use my voice, and discovering that ministry doesn't end when one door closes.

God opened new paths in children's ministry, storytelling, and the platform of social media where I can still share my testimony and help others meet Him through the very life He redeemed. I hope one day I will sing again. But if I don't, I will never lose faith in the God who saved me, sustained me, and gave me purpose again.

God took a girl who once lived recklessly, who once believed her life didn't matter very much and transformed her into someone who lives to remind others that *their* life absolutely does.

My purpose is no longer about success; it's about surrender. It's waking up every day and asking, "Lord, how can I be a light for You today?"

You may not have all the answers yet, and that's okay. You don't need to see the whole map when you trust the One who's holding it. God's purpose for your life will always unfold at the right pace.

You are not behind. You are right where He needs you to be for this moment.

Practical Steps to Live with Purpose

1. Start with prayer. Ask God each morning, "*How can I serve You today?*"
2. Identify your gifts. What comes naturally to you? What brings you joy? These are often clues to your calling.
3. Serve where you are. Purpose doesn't wait for perfect timing. Begin right where you are at home, at work, in your community.
4. Stay rooted in truth. Read Scripture daily to stay aligned with God's direction instead of the world's distractions.
5. Be patient. Purpose unfolds over time. Trust the process and stay faithful in small things.

Reflection

What gifts has God placed in your life? How can you use them to serve others and glorify Him? Write down one step you can take this week toward living with greater purpose.

Ask God to open your eyes to opportunities around you, moments where your presence, kindness, or words could change someone's day.

Prayer

Father, thank You for creating me with intention and purpose. Show me how to use my gifts to serve others and glorify You. Help me to stay focused on Your will and not be distracted by the lies of the enemy. Remind me that my life has meaning, that my story has value, and that You have prepared good works in advance for me to do. Give me the courage to walk in obedience, even when I don't see the full picture. Amen.

Verse

"For we are God's handiwork, created in Christ Jesus to do good works, which God prepared in advance for us to do."

— Ephesians 2:10 (NIV)

Chapter Twelve

The Journey Ahead

Your journey of renewing your mind doesn't end with the last page of this book, it begins here. The steps you've taken to identify lies, replace them with truth, and lean on God's Word are the foundation of a transformed life. But transformation is a daily walk, one that will continue as long as you draw breath.

I know what it feels like to wonder if change is possible. I spent nearly a decade trapped in cycles of pain, addiction, and lies. I tried to fix myself a hundred different ways, but freedom never came until I surrendered everything to God. His grace met me in the ruins of my old life and began to rebuild me piece by piece.

My story is living proof that the Holy Spirit still transforms hearts today. And if He did it for me, someone who thought she had gone too far, failed too many times, and was beyond repair, then He can do it for you too.

Choosing Daily Faithfulness

The key to lasting transformation isn't in one emotional moment: it's in choosing daily faithfulness. It's not about perfection, it's about persistence.

Renew your mind every day through prayer, Scripture, and gratitude. These are not rituals to check off a list, they are lifelines that connect you to the heart of God. When you pray, you are inviting Heaven to speak into your thoughts. When you read His Word, you are feeding your spirit with truth that drowns out the noise of the world. And when you give thanks, you are reminding your heart of all that God has already done.

There will be days when the old lies try to creep back in. Days when you feel unworthy or weary. But now you know what to do. You stand firm in truth. You put on the armor of God daily, knowing you are in a battle, but also knowing you fight from victory, not for it.

Ephesians 6 reminds us that our battle is not against flesh and blood, but against spiritual forces that want to steal our peace. The armor of God is truth, righteousness, faith, salvation, the Word, and prayer is your divine protection. Don't leave it hanging in the closet. Wear it every day.

Even when you don't *feel* strong, remember: your strength doesn't come from how you feel, it comes from who you belong to.

Staying Connected

God did not design us to walk this journey alone. He created community because transformation grows stronger in connection.

Surround yourself with people who will encourage you, challenge you, and remind you of God's truth. Find a church family, a small group, or a few trusted friends who can pray with you, hold you accountable, and celebrate your victories.

For a long time, I thought I had to do everything on my own. I didn't want to burden anyone with my struggles or let people see my flaws. But isolation is one of the enemy's favorite weapons. When you walk alone, you become an easy target.

Healing began for me when I started to open up. When I stopped pretending and let people in. God used others to speak life into me when I couldn't speak it to myself. Community became the mirror that helped me see the reflection of God's grace when I forgot who I was.

You don't have to be surrounded by perfect people; you just need people who point you back to Jesus.

Walking with Eternal Perspective

This world will always have struggles, distractions, and temptations. You will have good days and hard days. But your hope is not in this world, it's in Christ.

When you live with eternity in mind, daily challenges lose their power to shake you. You begin to realize that every step of obedience, every moment of surrender, every prayer whispered in faith is preparing you for something greater than this life.

Philippians 3:14 says, *"I press on toward the goal to win the prize for which God has called me heavenward in Christ Jesus."*

Walking with eternal perspective means keeping your eyes fixed on Jesus even when the road feels long. It means remembering that your pain is temporary, but your purpose is eternal.

Every trial you've faced has prepared you for the testimony you carry. Every scar tells the story of grace. And every victory (no matter how small) is evidence that the same God who began a good work in you is still at work today.

When you walk with eternity in your heart, even your hardest days have meaning.

When the Old Tries to Return

Renewing your mind doesn't make life suddenly easy, it makes you spiritually equipped. There will be moments when the old habits, fears, or temptations try to revisit you. But freedom means you no longer have to answer the door.

When the past calls, let it go to voicemail. You've already been redeemed.

You might stumble, but you won't stay down. You might doubt, but you won't despair. Why? Because now you know who you are and whose you are.

The enemy will always whisper reminders of who you used to be, but God will always speak louder about who you've become.

When lies say, *"You'll never change,"* truth says, *"You're already new."*

When shame says, *"You've gone too far,"* grace says, *"You're never out of reach."*

When fear says, *"You can't,"* faith says, *"With God, I can."*

A Personal Reflection

As I look back over this journey from addiction and hopelessness to renewal and freedom, I can see God's fingerprints on every page. He took what the enemy meant for destruction and used it for His glory.

There was a time when I thought my story was over. I thought I had wasted too many years and hurt too many people. But God didn't just redeem my life, He gave it purpose.

Now I wake up each morning with gratitude and awe, knowing I am living proof that God's grace still transforms. I am no longer a product of my past; I am a reflection of His promise.

And I want you to know this: the same power that restored me lives in you. The same grace that lifted me out of addiction can lift you out of fear, doubt, depression, or whatever chain tries to hold you.

You are not a lost cause. You are a chosen child of God, destined to walk in freedom and purpose.

Practical Steps for the Road Ahead

1. Stay rooted in Scripture. Keep feeding your mind with God's truth. His Word is your anchor when life tries to shake you.
2. Keep a gratitude journal. Writing down blessings shifts your focus from what's missing to what God is doing.
3. Pray often, even simply. Prayer doesn't have to be perfect; it just has to be honest. Talk to God like you would a close friend.
4. Find your people. Walk with those who remind you of your identity in Christ.
5. Celebrate progress. You may not be where you want to be but thank God you're not where you used to be.

Reflection

What step will you take today to continue renewing your mind? Write down one habit, one truth, or one practice that will keep you walking closer to God.

Think about the person you're becoming. Every decision, every prayer, every act of faith is shaping the life God has designed for you.

Prayer

Father, thank You for leading me through this journey of transformation. Thank You for the freedom, healing, and clarity You've brought into my life. As I step into the days ahead, remind me daily to renew my mind with Your truth. Help me to walk in freedom, live with purpose, and shine Your light to others. Keep my heart anchored in eternity and my eyes fixed on You. Amen.

Verse

"Being confident of this, that he who began a good work in you will carry it on to completion until the day of Christ Jesus."

— Philippians 1:6 (NIV)

Closing Words

As you finish these pages, remember this: your journey doesn't end here, it begins here. Renewing your mind is not a one-time choice but a daily walk with God. The battles may still come, and the lies may still whisper, but now you are equipped with His truth and His armor.

My prayer is that this book has reminded you of who you are in Christ: chosen, loved, redeemed, and set free. You don't have to fight with your own strength anymore. The same God who lifted me out of darkness is with you right now, ready to guide you every step of the way.

When fear rises, put on the armor of God.

When lies creep in, silence them with His Word.

When weakness overwhelms you, lean on His strength.

Your story is not over. In fact, it's just beginning. Go forward boldly, carrying the truth of God in your heart and sharing His light with the world.

"Finally, be strong in the Lord and in his mighty power.
Put on the full armor of God, so that you can take your stand
against the devil's schemes."

— Ephesians 6:10–11 (NIV)

About the Author

Joy was born in 1982 and has lived in Florida her entire life, raised in a warm and loving home by two devoted parents. Joy's parents met in college in the 70s, and together they raised two daughters in an atmosphere of love and togetherness. Her older sister is a proud mom of two handsome smart young men, while Joy is blessed to be the mother of two beautiful, sweet girls.

Although Joy was not consistently grounded in Scripture as a child, she never stopped loving God, family, and her family never stopped loving her. Her life's journey was far from perfect… marked by mistakes, wrong voices, and unseen spiritual battles, but God's grace met her where she was. When Joy surrendered fully to Him over 10 years ago, everything changed, and she never looked back.

In 2017 she met her husband, and by 2018 they were married and celebrating the arrival of their first miracle daughter, Lily. Five years later, their family grew again with the birth of another miracle, Savannah in 2023. Motherhood had always been Joy's deepest prayer, and God answered abundantly.

Today, Joy is passionate about helping others see God's blessings rather than curses, and to trust Him in the middle of life's struggles. Through her writing, she shares her story of redemption to encourage others: let God meet you where you are, give Him your wounds, and allow Him to bring healing and freedom. Joy is living proof that miracles happen… if you open your heart and let Him in.

www.ingramcontent.com/pod-product-compliance
Lightning Source LLC
LaVergne TN
LVHW010841120826
845149LV00020B/3432

* 9 7 9 8 9 9 5 2 3 4 8 0 7 *